THE AMERICAN
CITIZEN'S CREED

The American Citizen's Creed
Mending Our Country's Divide by Fostering Unity and Identity Among Citizens

Copyright 2025 Douglas M. Hammer
Dallas, Texas

https://www.anvil-cs.com/

ISBN 979-8-9935959-1-7

ISBN 979-8-9935959-2-4 (epub)

Cover photo by Gemini AI. (2025, November 3). American Citizen Creed Book Cover. Douglas Hammer, Author.

THE AMERICAN CITIZEN'S CREED

Mending Our Country's Divide by Fostering
Unity and Identity Among Citizens

COLONEL DOUGLAS M. HAMMER

For my children and grandchildren who represent the future citizens of our great country.

The United States wisely, freely, and liberally offers its citizenship to all who may come in good faith to reside within its limits on their complying with certain prescribed reasonable and simple formalities and conditions. Among the highest duties of the Government is that to afford firm, sufficient, and equal protection to all its citizens, whether native born or naturalized.

- President Ulysses S. Grant, 1874

Nothing is more important to America than citizenship; there is more assurance of our future in the individual character of our citizens than in any proposal I, and all the wise advisers I can gather, can ever put into effect in Washington.

- President Warren G. Harding, 1920

There is no more precious possession today than United States citizenship. A nation is no stronger than its citizenry. With many problems facing us daily in this perplexing and trying era, it is vital that we have a unity of purpose—to the end that freedom, justice, and opportunity, good will, and happiness may be assured ourselves and peoples everywhere.

- President Harry S. Truman, 1948

Table of Contents

Introduction 11

Why Now? 15

What is a Citizen and Citizenship? 25

Why a Creed? 41

The American Citizen's Creed 47

Our Identity and Fundamental Commitment 51

Connection of Our Core Beliefs to Historical Values .. 57

Protecting Our Nation and Upholding Its Ideals 71

Declaration of Our Commitment 81

Wrap-up 93

Quotes on Citizenship 97

About the Author 106

Introduction

Americans love our freedom. For some, it feels like the universal religion of our country.

The core idea I want to share in this book is simple: the amazing freedoms and privileges we're guaranteed as US citizens should spark a sense of responsibility, not entitlement. This is exactly what I believe President John F. Kennedy meant when he said "with privilege goes responsibility." [1]

Freedom Isn't Free

We often hear the saying "freedom isn't free" when talking about the sacrifices our military makes, and rightfully so. But that idea should apply to every single person who calls themselves a citizen of this great country. Our rights are a gift that demands something back from us. Yet, when we neglect this shared civic duty, the consequences become immediately visible in the fractured social fabric of our nation.

Douglas M. Hammer

The Great Divide

Over my sixty-one years, and especially in the last decade or so, I've watched Americans become more and more polarized—divided by where we live, what we believe, and who we vote for. This widening gap has damaged our social connections and destroyed trust, making it so much harder to solve common problems and build real community.

A 2024 study by the National Opinion Research Center at the University of Chicago[2] confirmed some good news: we still have things in common! The bad news? It's a deep and growing distrust of the government, the media, and even our fellow citizens. That last part—losing faith in each other—should really trouble us.

A lot of people point the finger at political leaders, who often seem to benefit by highlighting our differences instead of our similarities. But regardless of who's to blame, if we want to heal this national divide, we as citizens have to take responsibility for changing it. We need to focus on the positive qualities we share as Americans.

My Motivation for the Creed

My motivation for writing this book comes down to four main things:

1. My deep belief in and love for freedom.

Introduction

2. My passion for helping others become the best versions of themselves.
3. My agreement with President Ronald Reagan's serious warning that freedom is always just one generation away from being lost.
4. The growing polarization and divide I see in our country today.

The American Citizen's Creed is my attempt to highlight the common traits anyone who claims US citizenship should strive to embody. By focusing on these principles, my wish is for my children, and especially my grandchildren, to live in a more tolerant, peaceful, and connected America.

My sincere hope is that we can rally around our shared love of freedom and use it as a bridge to span our differences. I truly believe that despite all the noise and division, we still have so much in common. Let's make that our focus.

A quick spoiler: if you view citizenship as simply a matter of entitlement, this creed is probably not for you. But if, like me, you believe our freedoms aren't a free pass, then I hope you enjoy it.

Endnotes

1. John F. Kennedy Presidential Library, Remarks at Amherst College, Amherst, Massachusetts, October 26, 1963, https://www.jfklibrary.org/archives/other-resources/john-f-kennedy-speeches/amherst-college-19631026

2. NORC is one of the few trusted, nonpartisan research organizations with the sophistication, scientific rigor, and multidisciplinary teams of researchers—to execute this caliber of research.

Why Now?

As I mentioned before, that 2024 study found that Americans share a deep and growing distrust of the government, the media, and most troubling of all, each other. If we keep going down this road, where does it lead us?

Polarization and Violence

One seriously worrying result of this divide is the rise in violence against our fellow citizens. The numbers are alarming. The FBI reports that hate crimes have shot up 250 percent over the last ten years, with some spikes as high as 500 percent.

Additionally, political scientist James Piazza's 2020 study found hate speech by politicians directly boosts domestic terrorism.[1] Terrorism isn't just random violence; it's the deliberate use of violence (or the threat of it) for a political goal, meant to influence an audience far beyond the immediate victims.

Douglas M. Hammer

Piazza's work showed that this violence is facilitated by political polarization. In other words, when politicians use hate speech, they deepen the societal divisions and that, in turn, leads to more frequent domestic terrorism. The scale of this impact is jaw-dropping: countries where politicians used hate speech "often" or "extremely often" saw domestic attacks at nearly nine times the rate of countries where they used it "rarely" or "never."

Of course, our political leaders are always quick to condemn violence, but then they all too often go right back to the very rhetoric that fuels that behavior. The bottom line is, it's not enough for politicians to just denounce violence; they need the courage to look at their own words, acknowledge their role in the division, and actively work to stop the hate at its root. If they don't, they're essentially supporting the widening of the gap.

Another driver of polarization and violence amongst citizens can be explained by the cognitive bias called motive attribution asymmetry (MAA).[2] MAA is the tendency for individuals or groups to attribute their own motives differently from an opposing group's motives, especially in the context of conflict. MAA is basically a fancy term for a simple, yet destructive, human bias; we automatically assume the worst about people who don't think like we do. During times of conflict, we tend to attribute our own aggressive actions to love of our group and the opposing group's actions to hate of our group. Believing an opponent is grounded in hate or evil makes active listening and empathy impossible, leading to dehumanization and intractable conflict. We are bombarded with MAA constantly from our elected officials and the media, driving us more to violence rather than civil engagement. The consequences of this politically fueled cycle of MAA have become so severe that they have drawn urgent condemnation and a plea for civility from figures across the political spectrum.

During his testimony to the House Subcommittee Hearing on the Weaponization of the Federal Government,[3] then-presidential candidate Robert F. Kennedy Jr. had these comments about how toxic polarization is destroying our country today. "This kind of division is more dangerous for our country than any time since the American Civil War. How do we deal with that? How are we…to end that polarization. Do you think you can do that by censoring people? I'm telling you, you cannot. That only aggregates and amplifies the problem. We need to start being kind to each other. We need to start being respectful to each other. We need to start restoring the comity to this Chamber and to the rest of America, but it has to start here."

He went on to say, "Debate, congenial respectful debate is the fertilizer. It's the water. It's the sunlight for our democracy. We need to be talking to each other. We need to be able to talk--and the First Amendment was not written for easy speech. It was written for the speech that nobody likes you for." He concluded his statement by saying, "We have to stop trying to destroy each other, to marginalize, to vilify, to gaslight each other. We have to find a place inside of ourselves, a light of empathy, of compassion. Above all, we need to elevate the Constitution of the United States, which was written for hard times, and that has to be the premier compass for all our activities."

Bridging this polarization isn't just the responsibility of our elected officials. As citizens, we need to hold them accountable, but we also have to resist letting extremists on either side pull us over the edge toward violence. That's why I believe a creed is necessary—it provides a foundation for citizens to anchor ourselves to.

Diminishing Consent of the Governed

Another reason we need a creed is rooted in our Declaration of Independence.

We know the famous line: "We hold these truths to be self-evident, that all men are created equal... endowed by their Creator with certain unalienable Rights, that among these are Life, Liberty, and the pursuit of Happiness." But many do not remember the next sentence. "That to secure these rights, Governments are instituted among Men, deriving their just powers from the consent of the governed."

While many Americans can recite our unalienable rights, fewer realize the Declaration also lays out the plan for what should happen when the government no longer supports those principles. It states that "whenever any Form of Government becomes destructive of these ends, it is the Right of the People to alter or abolish it, and to institute new Government, laying its foundation on such principles and organizing its powers in such form, as to them shall seem most likely to effect their Safety and Happiness."

Our founders, being wise to human nature, also included a caution within the Declaration of Independence: we shouldn't change a long-established government "for light and transient causes." Although we're naturally more inclined to just suffer through manageable evils, our founders were clear that when citizens experience "a long train of abuses and usurpations" that points toward tyranny, "it is their right, it is their duty, to throw off such Government."

Here are a few quick takeaways I have about the Declaration:

1. It is the Declaration of Independence, not the Declaration of Dependence. An entitled view of citizenship, which implies dependency, is completely contradictory to freedom.
2. Liberty is the state of being free from oppressive restrictions on our life and behavior.
3. Happiness is not a right in our country—only the pursuit of it. That means it's not the government's job, or our neighbor's, to make us happy.

4. One of our most fundamental rights is to alter or abolish the government when it becomes destructive. But this right comes with the caution that we shouldn't act rashly or for "light and transient causes."

Let me be absolutely clear: I am not suggesting we should abolish our government and start over. When we look at the political landscape, we see everything from groups focused on simple governmental reform to others working to alter the Constitution itself through methods like an Article V Convention. It's only on the very fringes, among groups like anarchists or revolutionary socialists, where you find people truly calling for abolition—a total restart. But I do recognize that some groups feel this is the answer, and their existence should be a warning sign about our current state.

What I am suggesting is that we need to alter our course by focusing on our common, founding principles and holding leaders accountable when they promote division over unity. One simple way to exercise our right to alter our government is by replacing the elected officials who comprise it. We can organize and use our votes to elect people who actually support our founding and common principles.

My fear is that if we continue down this path of polarization, the more extreme option of abolishing the government gains momentum. More and more citizens will stop seeing the division and violence as "light and transient" and start seeing it as "a long train of abuses and usurpations, designed to reduce them under absolute despotism."

Declining of the Civic Mission of Schools

A healthy democracy absolutely depends on informed and engaged citizens. This isn't just a nice thought—it's an essential ingredient. In a government of the people, by the people, and for the people, the ultimate power rests with us. Our government will only be as good as we demand it to be. If citizens check out and fail to demand accountability, we open the door for crises, abuse of power, and special interest groups to gain too much influence. To safeguard our system against such failures, we must cultivate the informed dialogue and critical thinking required for self-governance.

Civic education is vital for teaching us how to have constructive public dialogue in our diverse society. When everything is dominated by partisanship and ideology, productive discussions stop. Without a strong grounding in civics, people can easily fall for misinformation. Civic education is the antidote, empowering us to combat false narratives and think critically about issues.

So, how is civic education doing in American schools?

According to a key 2011 report, Guardian of Democracy, The Civic Mission of Schools,[4] the state of civic learning is inadequate, leading to a poorly informed citizenry. They

Douglas M. Hammer

found that two-thirds of American students scored below proficient on a national civics assessment, and shockingly, less than one-third of eighth graders could identify the historic purpose of the Declaration of Independence. One major reason? Schools often treat civics as an elective, not a core subject.

That report also highlighted that challenges like growing distrust, a divided citizenry, and increasing polarization could all be addressed through better civic education. Failing to adequately prepare future generations to tackle these challenges collaboratively ultimately hinders effective governance. Though that study is fourteen years old, more recent surveys to include the 2022 survey conducted by the Annenberg Public Policy Center and the May 2024 American Bar Association's The State of Civics Education in the General Populace, have shown that the data is only getting worse. We can see the deterioration of our civic health not only in failing test results but also in the way we've abandoned simple, shared, national rituals.

I feel a causal factor in this decline is the drop in reciting the Pledge of Allegiance—not just in schools, but by adults at public events. For many birthright citizens, reciting the Pledge is the closest we'll ever come to taking an oath. Remember, we are not just pledging allegiance to our flag, but also to "the republic for which it stands." The Pledge is a public reaffirmation that we are "one nation under God, indivisible, with liberty and justice for all." Reciting

Why Now?

the Pledge at more public events would give Americans another shared action to rally around and remind us of our common beliefs. The urgency of this moment in time—marked by polarization, growing distrust, violence, and the decline of civic education—demands a clear framework for unity and are all signs that the time for *The American Citizen's Creed* is now.

Before I articulate the proposed creed, let's return to the most basic premise. What, fundamentally, does it mean to be a citizen, and what is the true nature of American citizenship?

Douglas M. Hammer

Endnotes

1. Piazza, J. A. (2020). Politician hate speech and domestic terrorism. International Interactions, 46(3), 431–453. https://doi.org/10.1080/03050629.2020.1739033

2. Morgan, Karina (2025, April 7) "We shouldn't assume bad intent from those we disagree with." The Ethics Centre,https://ethics.org.au/we-shouldnt-assume-bad-intent-from-those-we-disagree-with/

3. The Weaponization of the Federal Government, House Hearing, 118 Congress (Thursday, July 20, 2023) (The Honorable Robert F. Kennedy Jr.) https://www.congress.gov/event/118th-congress/house-event/116258/text

4. Gould, J., Jamieson, K. H., Levine, P., McConnell, T., & Smith, D. B. (2011). Guardian of democracy: The civic mission of schools. Philadelphia: The Lenore Annenberg Institute for Civics of the Annenberg Public Policy Center of the University of Pennsylvania, and the Campaign for the Civic Mission of Schools.

What is a Citizen and Citizenship?

This Creed is for anyone who calls themselves a citizen. But what exactly does it mean to be a citizen? And what is citizenship? To answer those questions, let's take a look at history.

Citizenship in Early Western Civilization

As I recall from my Western Civilization classes back at the University of Arkansas, the idea of citizenship first emerged all the way back in the city-states of ancient Greece. From the very beginning, citizenship meant freedom and protection, but it came with responsibilities.

A citizen in a Greek city-state was protected by the government, got to vote, and was expected to pay taxes and perform military service. The catch? Not everyone was a citizen—slaves, peasants, women, and resident foreigners were just subjects. For those privileged who were citizens, being a good citizen was crucial. Participation wasn't just a right; it was seen as a duty. A citizen who shirked responsibilities was considered a disruptive force in society.

The Romans later used citizenship (civitas) primarily as a way to distinguish the people living in Rome from those in the lands they conquered. Roman citizenship was a privileged political and legal status for free individuals, giving them rights concerning laws, property, and governance. It was complex, but it basically boiled down to a relationship. The individual owed allegiance to the state, and in turn, the state owed the individual protection.

Citizenship in the Early United States

Fast forward about 1,300 years to the birth of the United States. Our founding documents give us a clear view of how our early leaders saw citizenship.

The Articles of Confederation (our first constitution, used until 1789) talked about the "free inhabitants" of each State being entitled to "all privileges and immunities of free citizens." Interestingly, the Articles did specifically exclude "paupers, vagabonds, and fugitives from justice" from these privileges. While that sounds harsh by modern standards, we have to look at the context.

Paupers weren't just the poor; they were people deemed permanently incapable of caring for themselves. Vagabonds were people with no established residence. Even today, you have to establish residency somewhere to vote. I'm not

What is a Citizen and Citizenship?

saying these exceptions were right, but they clearly show that our Founders believed not all people should have all privileges—drawing a distinction between citizens and others who resided in our country.

Because the Articles of Confederation led to a confusing lack of uniformity in citizenship policies, it helped push the nation toward drafting the US Constitution. The Constitution, in Article IV, Section 2, stated that "citizens of each state shall be entitled to all the privileges and immunities of citizens in the several states," but didn't list those exceptions in the Articles of Confederation.

The big change came much later with the Fourteenth Amendment (1868), which clarified citizenship for good: "All persons born or naturalized in the United States, and subject to the jurisdiction thereof, are citizens of the United States and of the State wherein they reside."

A naturalized citizen is a lawful permanent resident who is granted citizenship after meeting the requirements established by Congress in the Immigration and Nationality Act (INA).

The Fourteenth Amendment also guaranteed that no state could deny citizens their rights without due process of law or deny any person the equal protection of the laws.

Here are my key takeaways from our founders' views on citizenship:

1. Citizens are defined as persons born or naturalized in the United States.
2. The Founders originally believed that not all people should have all privileges, which created a distinction between citizens and non-citizens/residents.
3. Thanks to the Fourteenth Amendment, simply being accused is not enough to deny someone their privileges; you must follow the due process of law.

Looking at the history, it's clear that citizenship has always been a fundamental contract: a set of rights and a set of duties.

A Modern View of Citizenship

To understand how the concept of citizenship has changed over the years, let's look at a modern view. You can think of it in two main ways: the legal view and the feeling of belonging.

The Legal View. The first, and probably the most common view, is the legality of citizenship. This is the formal, legal relationship that gives us specific rights and privileges (like voting or protection), but it also comes with essential responsibilities or civic duties (like following laws). It's a classic two-way street: the country protects us and our interests, and in return, we have obligations to our country.

What is a Citizen and Citizenship?

The Feeling of Belonging. But citizenship is so much more than just a legal status; it's also about a feeling of belonging. It's about being part of a community we can actually influence and shape. A community can be defined in all sorts of ways—maybe it's a group with shared values, a set of common rights, or just a shared identity. Geographically, this could be our neighborhood, our town, or our entire nation.

The Citizenship Stool. Another way to really understand how a citizen fits into society is to look at citizenship like a four-legged stool (see Figure 2.1), as defined by the Council of Europe.[1] To be a well-rounded citizen, we need to keep all four legs in balance. If one is taken away, the stool topples.

Figure 2.1. Four-Legged Stool of Citizenship

- Political Leg: This covers our rights and responsibilities within our political system. It's about understanding how government works and knowing how to participate, whether by voting or getting involved in a local cause.
- Social Leg: This is about how we interact with others. It involves being loyal and showing solidarity with the

people around us. It requires strong social skills to build good relationships within our community.
- Cultural Leg: This is our connection to our shared history and heritage. It means knowing our culture and history, and having basic skills like reading and writing so we can actually engage with it all.
- Economic Leg: This is our relationship with the economy and job market. It includes the right to work and to have a basic standard of living. This leg is all about having the skills and training needed to contribute.

These different parts of citizenship aren't things we're born with; they're learned. We pick them up from our families and friends, at school and throughout our communities. Ultimately, citizenship is an active practice. It's about getting involved and working to make our community— whether that's our neighborhood, our country, or the world—better. This idea of active citizenship is all about contributing to the well-being of everyone.

Categorization of Citizens

Another interesting way to look at citizenship is taken from Daniel Miessler's essay, The Hierarchy of Citizenship.[2]

CITIZENS are what we should all become. To be a Citizen constitutes both the minimum and the maximum. They represent the lifeforce of a country, as they are the

What is a Citizen and Citizenship?

ones thinking, discussing, and holding accountable those who would lead us. Citizens:

- Are employed
- Have opinions that may deviate from their group
- Maintain considerable knowledge of how the world works
- Know and interact with their representatives
- Vote according to issues

COGS, along with Citizens, form the backbone of functioning societies. Unlike citizens, Cogs are not questioning and contemplating their opinions, and are making them based on group dynamics for the most part, but they are at least engaged in the process even if it is from within a box. Cogs:

- Are employed
- Have the opinion of their group
- Maintain a decent understanding of how the world works
- May know and interacted with their representatives
- Vote obediently according to party

ACCESSORIES are arguably the most detrimental group to a society because they look from the outside like they might be Cogs or Citizens, but they're much more like Barnacles. They work and pay taxes and are therefore much more practically useful than the Barnacles who don't, but they do these things mostly because it's the accepted thing to do, not out of principle. Accessories:

- Are employed
- Have no political opinions
- Have little or no understanding of how the world works
- Don't know or interact with their representatives
- Do not vote

BARNACLES (Passengers) are those who pull upon society without giving back. They consume the benefits of a given society and culture, but they do not contribute. They don't work. They enroll in public programs, consume food paid for by the cogs and the citizens, often complaining all the while about how broken the system is. Barnacles:

- Are willfully unemployed
- Have no political opinions
- Have little or no knowledge of the world
- Don't know or interact with their representatives
- Do not vote

I agree with Miessler's core belief: "What the United States—and arguably every country—needs more than anything else is citizens. This should not be confused with people who have citizenship, as in too many cases these have little in common."

Miessler makes a powerful point about active citizenship and how many people who have the status of citizenship fail to actually achieve it. His framework offers a helpful way to visualize the difference between various roles people play in society.

While many may disagree with Miessler's labels or descriptions, I feel his view of citizenship does agree with the Articles of Confederation's notion that "paupers, vagabonds, and fugitives from justice" were distinct from "citizens." It's also helpful in highlighting the differences in how groups of Americans view their responsibilities as citizens. For example, Miessler's Barnacle and Accessory are what I called out within the Introduction as having an entitlement view of citizenship. Like Miessler, I agree that to call yourself a Citizen we must acknowledge that our rights come with responsibilities.

Birthright Citizenship: The Fourteenth Amendment

The Fourteenth Amendment to the Constitution states: "All persons born or naturalized in the United States, and subject to the jurisdiction thereof, are citizens of the United States."

Douglas M. Hammer

Proponents of birthright citizenship say this simple line covers almost everyone born on US soil. Regardless of these views or the intense political debate, the current legal reality is that anyone born on US soil is considered a citizen.

Birthright citizenship fosters societal cohesion. It integrates children of immigrants and prevents a marginalized, hereditary underclass. It also simplifies things dramatically: our birth certificate is our proof of citizenship. It guarantees equal opportunity and fairness, creating an inclusive democracy where citizenship isn't determined by our race, family line, or parents' status.

With all the benefits of birthright citizenship, there are people who exploit it. We've heard of "birth tourism," where people come to the US specifically to give birth so their child can get US citizenship. Entering on a tourist visa with that primary intent is actually visa fraud, which is illegal but tough to prove, and the child born here is still legally a US citizen. The parents' motivation is often that having a US citizen child can help them when they later ask for "deferred action," which is temporary protection from deportation.

Some countries are reacting to this with restricted birthright citizenship. Countries like Australia, France, Ireland, New Zealand, and the United Kingdom now require at least one parent to be a citizen or legal permanent resident

What is a Citizen and Citizenship?

for the child to gain citizenship. In the US, there are many who support restricted birthright citizenship. They argue the Fourteenth Amendment was never meant to cover the children of parents who are here illegally or on temporary visas.Beyond the strict legal definition, this cornerstone principle is vital for fostering national unity and guaranteeing equality for everyone born here.

The Naturalization Process: Citizenship Isn't Easy

If you want proof that citizenship comes with responsibilities, just look at our naturalization process. It's anything but easy. Prospective citizens have to jump through a lot of hoops to include subjecting themselves to a moral character review, passing an English and civics test, and taking an oath of allegiance.

Moral Character Review. Applicants have to prove they are a person of "good moral character" and are attached to the principles of the Constitution. This is much more comprehensive than a simple background check. It's a holistic review of an applicant's behavior and adherence to societal norms. A clean criminal record isn't enough anymore. Our government looks at the applicant's:

- Behavior and Conduct: Is your overall life consistent with current ethical standards?

- Wider Factors: They check community involvement, education, employment, financial history, and even online/social media activity.
- Disqualifying Behavior: They can even look at technically lawful behaviors deemed inconsistent with civic responsibility, like habitual traffic infractions or harassment.

English and Civics Tests. Applicants have to take an English test to prove they can read, write, and speak the language. Additionally, they also have to pass a civics test to confirm they understand the fundamentals of US history and government. The civics test has a pool of 128 questions. Applicants are asked up to twenty questions and must answer twelve correctly to pass. The questions are complex and require a deeper understanding, not just simple memorization.

The Oath of Allegiance. Finally, naturalized citizens must also take an Oath of Allegiance in which they declare they will "support and defend the Constitution and laws of the United States of America against all enemies, foreign and domestic; that I will bear true faith and allegiance to the same."

To "bear true faith and allegiance" to the Constitution means to have complete belief in its goodness and to offer unwavering loyalty to it as the supreme law of the land. It signifies a commitment to uphold its principles, defend it

What is a Citizen and Citizenship?

against all enemies, and act in accordance with its laws and the values it embodies.

Faith involves a deep and sincere belief that the Constitution and its principles are right and good. It is a belief in the fundamental ideals of liberty, equality, and justice that the Constitution represents. Allegiance refers to complete and steadfast loyalty. When we bear allegiance, we are giving our devoted commitment to the Constitution. It's crucial to note that the oath says citizens will support and defend the Constitution, not a political leader, a specific party, or any other authority. Our loyalty is to the document that binds us all.

A final thought on the naturalization process. I feel every citizen should read *The Citizen's Almanac*[3] produced by the US Citizenship and Immigration Services which provides an overview of our fundamental documents, symbols, and anthems of the United States. If naturalized citizens must read it, all citizens *should* read it. This concept of shared civic ideals leads directly to how I view the population within the US—not as a simple split, but as a continuum of statuses.

Statuses Within the US

I see our population as a continuum. Visitors who can benefit from and contribute to our society should have a pathway to become Permanent Residents. Those Residents can then become legal Citizens by going through the naturalization process. Ultimately Citizens should aspire to Public Service. (Full transparency: my twenty-six years in the US Air Force biased me to believe that public servants represent the highest form of citizenry.)

VISITORS have temporary permission to enter and stay in the U.S. and possess basic legal protections but are subject to time limits and specific entry/exit rules.

PERMANENT RESIDENTS have the right to live and work permanently in the US, own property, and access some public benefits, along with constitutional rights like due process and equal protection under the law. However, they cannot vote or run for political office, and have restrictions on long-term travel abroad, and can be deported for certain actions.

CITIZENS hold full nationality and the highest level of rights and protections, including the right to vote, hold federal jobs, and are protected from deportation.

PUBLIC SERVANT is a subset of Citizens who honorably serve their fellow citizens with the primary goal of serving the public interest rather than personal gain. Includes military, firefighters, police officers, teachers, social workers, elected officials, etc.

What is a Citizen and Citizenship?

Summary of American Citizenship

- Privilege with Responsibility: No matter how we got here, citizenship should be viewed as a privilege that comes with civic responsibility.
- Civic Duty: This is the job of citizens to be active in society and genuinely consider the interests of others. We have an obligation to serve society, and in return, we get rights and protections.
- Aim Higher: Citizens should aspire to be more than just Miessler's barnacle, accessory, or cog. We should maximize our positive contribution to our communities and our nation. This starts with a solid foundation of American civics.

Having established the parameters of what a citizen and citizenship are, the obvious next question is how we, as citizens, can bridge our current political division. The answer lies not in more laws, but in a powerful, shared statement—a creed—designed to cut through polarization and reaffirm our most basic beliefs, reminding citizens about their privileges and duties.

Endnotes

1. Council of Europe, manual for Human Rights Education with Young People, Citizenship and Participation. https://www.coe.int/en/web/compass/citizenship-and-participation

2. Daniel Miessler (May 30, 2015), The Hierarchy of Citizenship, https://danielmiessler.com/blog/hierarchy-of-citizenship

3. U.S. Department of Homeland Security, U.S. Citizenship and Immigration Services, Office of Citizenship, The Citizen's Almanac, Washington, DC, 2014.

Why a Creed?

In simple terms, a creed is just a concise statement of core beliefs. Most people associate creeds with religion, but their purpose is actually much broader. They act as a unifying force, fostering a shared understanding and communal identity. Think of it this way: if the universal faith of the United States is liberty and freedom, shouldn't we have a creed to articulate our universal beliefs about what it means to be an American?

A good creed clarifies the core beliefs and complex ideas of citizenship, making them easier to understand. Defining a common set of principles promotes unity and fellowship, helping to foster a shared identity across all our communities. It's a fantastic educational tool for passing down foundational truths, and reciting it provides a vital historical connection to citizens both today and across time. Finally, a creed serves as an intellectual defense, setting clear boundaries to guard against ideas that stray too far from our core doctrine.

Douglas M. Hammer

Modernizing the *American's Creed* of 1917: From Obligation to Engagement

In 1917, amid the surge of World War I-era patriotism, William Tyler Page authored *The American's Creed* as part of a national contest designed to foster civic duty. Page, a dedicated public servant who worked in the US Capitol for sixty-one years (culminating as Clerk of the House of Representatives), possessed an intimate understanding of the nation's political tradition.

Page's winning entry aimed to be a brief, comprehensive summary of the fundamental principles of American political faith. He believed the nation, focused on its privileges, needed a timely reminder of its core obligations as citizens. Masterfully blending key phrases from formative documents—the Preamble, the Declaration of Independence, and the Gettysburg Address—his creed became a solemn declaration of duty to the state and its framework. It was officially adopted by the US House of Representatives on April 3, 1918.

The American's Creed (1917)

> I believe in the United States of America as a government of the people, by the people, for the people; whose just powers are derived from the consent of the governed, a democracy in a republic, a sovereign Nation of many sovereign States; a perfect union, one and inseparable;

established upon those principles of freedom, equality, justice, and humanity for which American patriots sacrificed their lives and fortunes.

I therefore believe it is my duty to my country to love it, to support its Constitution, to obey its laws, to respect its flag, and to defend it against all enemies.

While Page's creed highlights the foundational belief in self-governance and the corresponding obligation of the citizen, its focus—love, support, obey, respect, and defend—is largely directed toward the government and its symbols. This focus is insufficient for the complex, diverse, and polarized America of today.

The current national divide demonstrates that allegiance to the Constitution does not automatically translate into functional citizenship within the community. The traditional duties are passive, whereas a healthy modern-day democracy requires active, ethical engagement.

To make *The American's Creed* truly applicable and relevant today, we must modernize the concept of civic duty by including pillars of citizenship that extend beyond mere loyalty to the country and include both an interpersonal focus through the duty of civility and tolerance as well as robust civic participation through the duty of engagement and contribution.

Douglas M. Hammer

What I Learned in the Air Force

Creeds are incredibly powerful for unifying people and building community. I saw this firsthand during my time in the Air Force. As a commander, I made it a point to sit down over breakfast with every single one of the 1,300-plus airmen in the 86th Civil Engineer Group. One thing we always talked about was why we joined the Air Force. That breakfast taught me there were as many different reasons for joining as there were airmen.

The logical follow-up question I'd ask everyone was, "Why do you stay in the Air Force?"

I found the reasons for staying were much more universal and perfectly captured within our *Airman's Creed*:[1]

> I am an American Airman.
> I am a warrior.
> I have answered my nation's call.
>
>
> I am an American Airman.
> My mission is to fly, fight, and win.
> I am faithful to a proud heritage,
> A tradition of honor,
> And a legacy of valor.
>
> I am an American Airman,
> Guardian of freedom and justice,
> My nation's sword and shield,

Why a Creed?

> Its sentry and avenger.
> I defend my country with my life.
>
>
> I am an American Airman:
> Wingman, leader, warrior.
> I will never leave an Airman behind,
> I will never falter,
> And I will not fail.

The *Airman's Creed* is a short, memorable declaration of the values and principles that guide our airmen. It's designed to unify them under a common set of beliefs and inspire them to work toward a shared goal. As a continuous ritual, the creed is taught during basic military training and recited regularly at gatherings and formal ceremonies to ensure its message is ingrained in every airman. I watched this creed bring together a highly diverse group of Americans—different races, religions, socio-economic backgrounds, and ideological lines—into one cohesive unit. Knowing the Air Force is just a microcosm of our country, I feel a creed has the power to unify us as a nation.

Why *The American Citizen's Creed*?

As I thought about the growing polarization in America, I couldn't help but wonder: maybe we just need an American citizen's creed to highlight the common values and responsibilities we all share.

Endnotes

1. Introduced by General T. Michael Moseley, Chief of Staff of the Air Force, 2007

The American Citizen's Creed

Below is my proposal for *The American Citizen's Creed* organized into four stanzas.

> I am an American citizen.
> I am a patriot.
> My generation's defender of liberty.

> I am an American citizen.
> I honor and protect our founding principles.
> I abide by our laws and respect the rights, beliefs, and opinions of my fellow citizens.

> I am an American citizen.
> I stay informed of issues affecting my community and actively contribute to its well-being.
> I participate in the democratic process and serve in times of need.

> I am an American citizen.
> Proud patriot and protector.
> I practice accountability, civility, and tolerance.
> I reject violence as a way of settling differences.
> I protect and maintain my rights by exercising my responsibilities.

Douglas M. Hammer

The first stanza establishes our identity and our fundamental commitment as citizens.

> **I am an American citizen.**
> **I am a patriot.**
> **My generation's defender of liberty.**

The second stanza expands on our core beliefs and their connection to our historical values.

> **I am an American citizen.**
> **I honor and protect our founding principles.**
> **I abide by our laws and respect the rights, beliefs, and opinions of my fellow citizens.**

The third stanza highlights our role in being engaged in our communities and actively participating both local and national levels to contribute positively to its well-being.

> **I am an American citizen.**
> **I stay informed of issues affecting my community and actively contribute to its well-being.**
> **I participate in the democratic process and serve in times of need.**

The final stanza reiterates our role as Americans and concludes with strong declaration of our commitment to the country and our fellow citizens.

The American Citizen's Creed

**I am an American citizen.
Proud patriot and protector of our Constitution.
I practice accountability, civility, and tolerance.
I reject violence as a way of settling differences.
I protect and maintain my rights by exercising my
responsibilities.**

Reciting the creed is about affirming not just the qualities we as citizens have but also those we should aspire to. The creed is both a journey and a destination.

Our Identity and Fundamental Commitment

I am an American citizen. I am a patriot. My generation's defender of liberty.

This first part of the creed is all about establishing who we are and our most basic commitment as citizens.

Patriot

The first key word here is "patriot." A patriot is someone who strongly supports their country and is ready to defend it against threats.

Defining the word is one thing; understanding what makes a good patriot is another. I base my characteristics on the ideas of political philosopher Stephen Nathanson.[1] A good patriot includes:

- Affection and loyalty: Having a special fondness for our country—its culture, traditions, and history—and wanting to protect and preserve it.
- Concern for the common good: Caring deeply about our country's welfare and wanting to contribute positively to its future and the lives of others.
- Willingness to sacrifice: Willingness to make personal sacrifices to promote our nation's values and prosperity. This could mean military service, voting, volunteering, or simply engaging in civic life.
- Informed and engaged citizenship: Not blindly following leaders. A patriot knows our country's history and government and actively participates in the democratic process. This includes holding leaders accountable and honestly addressing past national mistakes.
- Respect for fellow citizens: Treating other citizens as equals, showing them goodwill and respect, no matter their differences.
- Upholding national values: Upholding the fundamental values of the country, like freedom, justice, and equality, and constantly working to improve them.
- Humility and self-reflection: Acknowledging and learning from the country's past mistakes to build a better future.

It's important to understand the difference between patriotism and nationalism. While both involve love of country, nationalism often carries a sense of inherent superiority over other nations, while patriotism simply focuses on love of your own country without that supremacist belief.

Liberty

The second key term in the stanza is "liberty." When I use this term, I'm talking about the state of being free from oppressive restrictions and external control—being allowed to live, act, and think without undue interference from authority or others. It covers both the freedom to pursue our own goals within a lawful and fair system and those specific rights guaranteed in our Constitution and Bill of Rights. Key aspects of liberty include:

- Freedom from Authority: Being free from arbitrary government or social restrictions on our way of life.
- Freedom of Choice: The power to choose and act for ourself, to pursue our own tastes and beliefs as long as we don't harm others.
- Individual Sovereignty: The idea that we are sovereign over ourselves.
- Civil and Political Rights: Enjoying the same rights and privileges as everyone else in a free society.

My Generation's Defender of Liberty

I included the phrase "my generation's defender of liberty" to make a critical point: every generation either contributes

Douglas M. Hammer

to or degrades our liberty. We often talk about "The Greatest Generation" (those who came of age during the Great Depression and World War II) and how they shaped modern America through incredible civic engagement and sacrifice. They earned that label, and we should strive to contribute to our nation in our own time. Instead of constantly comparing our contributions to those of past generations, focus on what we can do right now to advance citizenship and safeguard liberty.

With that understanding of patriot and liberty, read the first stanza again. There's a powerful amount of meaning packed into those few words.

Defining our identity and fundamental commitment as Americans within the first stanza is a crucial first step, but it raises an immediate and essential question of content. What, precisely, are the shared tenets that will ground this commitment? We find the answer within the second stanza by defining our core beliefs and tracing their inseparable connection to the nation's historic values.

Endnotes

1. Patriotism, Morality, and Peace. Stephen Nathanson – 1993 – Rowman & Littlefield Publishers

The Connection of Our Core Beliefs to Historical Values

I am an American citizen. I honor and protect our founding principles. I abide by our laws and respect the rights, beliefs, and opinions of my fellow citizens.

This second stanza expands on our core beliefs and emphasizes their connection to America's historical values.

Honor and Protect our Founding Principles

A citizen holds the founding principles of the Declaration of Independence to be self-evident and defends the Constitutional rights of others even when those rights conflict with our personal and religious beliefs. This conviction, that all people are created equal, means the basic principles of humanity apply universally—not just to one group or nation, but to all of us.

Douglas M. Hammer

I realize that many find our founding principles to be outdated and even hypocritical, but before examining those arguments, let's remind ourselves of why they are worth defending.

1. They guard our rights and liberties. The founding documents set up the framework that protects our individual freedoms—like free speech, religious freedom, and freedom of the press. They are the essential guardrails against the government getting too big or stepping out of line. The whole concept of "unalienable rights" means these freedoms are inherent to us; they aren't just gifts granted by the government.
2. They ensure the rule of law. The idea that all citizens are equal under the law is the cornerstone of a fair society. It keeps leaders from being above the law and prevents the abuse of power. Protecting the founding structure—like the checks and balances—keeps the government accountable to us instead of letting it expand without limit.
3. They give us a shared identity. By committing to ideals like liberty and equality, we create a common national purpose that can unite very diverse people. For our republic to actually work, citizens need good civic habits like moderation, honesty, and a commitment to the public good. Honoring the principles encourages these habits.

The Connection of Our Core Beliefs to Historical Values

4. They allow for progress. The founding principles give us a standard to measure ourselves against. They act as a moral compass we can use to spot our nation's mistakes and work toward a more just society. Instead of being rigid, these ideals are an ongoing aspiration—the nation's strength comes from its ability to strive for a "more perfect union," even when we fall short.

We must acknowledge that not everyone agrees we should prioritize these principles, and critics raise very important counterarguments that are worth addressing. These counterarguments include the following:

1. The founders were hypocritical. It's impossible to ignore the historical contradiction. Many founders who preached "liberty and equality" also owned slaves. Critics argue this fundamental hypocrisy tarnishes the legacy and suggest the original political order was designed mainly by and for powerful men to protect their own interests.
2. The principles might be outdated. Some argue that the founders' ideas, particularly those rooted in classical liberalism, have actually led to negative outcomes in the modern world, like radical individualism, self-absorption, or ignoring the environment. This view suggests the principles are simply inadequate for today's complexities and adherence to them slows down necessary progress.

3. They cause conflict, not unity. Let's face it, people disagree wildly on what the founding principles actually mean and how they should be applied today. Instead of unifying us, these competing interpretations can become a major source of political conflict.

Despite those counterarguments, the case for honoring our founding principles is this: they are the language of our shared rights and the standard for our self-correction. We should honor them not because the founders were flawless, but because the principles themselves—liberty, equality, and unalienable rights—are the most powerful weapons we have against tyranny and injustice. They allow us to call out the nation's failures and demand a better future. When we protect the constitutional rights of others, even those we disagree with, we are simply ensuring that those rights will be there to protect us when we need them most. The principles aren't just history; they are the framework for our future freedom.

Abide By Our Laws

The second core belief addressed in this stanza is abiding by our laws. Okay, this one may be a no-brainer but still worth discussing because plenty of our fellow citizens do not believe in the rule of law or applying it equally. A good citizen respects the rights, beliefs, and opinions of others. We understand that if the rights of even one person are violated, the rights of all are at risk. We also

The Connection of Our Core Beliefs to Historical Values

respect the personal beliefs of others and don't try to force our own beliefs on them. We recognize that human rights are inherent—they belong to everyone just because they're human. This essential respect for the rights and humanity of all citizens is the starting point, but it requires a solid, shared, legal framework to be sustained.

Good citizens follow laws to create a stable, safe, and fair society for everyone. A solid legal system protects our individual rights, settles disputes without violence, and provides the basic order we need for a thriving life. The whole idea of the rule of law works only because most people are willing to follow the rules, even when no one is looking.

Laws aren't just there to punish us; they form the foundation of a good community by:

- Keeping Things Orderly: Imagine what would happen if people just disobeyed traffic laws whenever they wanted. Life would be chaotic and dangerous. Following laws is what keeps public safety intact and daily life running smoothly.
- Promoting Cooperation: Laws are part of a "social contract." We agree to obey certain rules in exchange for the benefits of an orderly society. This mutual agreement builds trust and makes sure society functions well for all.

- Protecting the Vulnerable: Laws set clear standards of behavior that prevent exploitation and harm, offering crucial protection to the most vulnerable members of our society.
- Fueling the Economy: A strong rule of law gives businesses confidence to invest and grow because they know contracts will be honored and corruption will be reduced. This is a direct path to economic growth and prosperity.
- Ensuring Fairness: Laws are designed to apply equally to everyone. This holds us accountable for our actions and ensures that everyone has equal access to justice.

Following the law is good for us personally too, because it results in:

- Protecting Our Rights: Our laws, especially the Constitution and Bill of Rights, protect your fundamental freedoms—like speech, religion, and property—from being taken away by either the government or other citizens.
- Keeping Us Safe: Rules for things like traffic, food safety, and medical licensing are all designed to protect you from physical harm.
- Giving Us a Path to Justice: When you are wronged, the legal system provides a formal, peaceful way for you to seek justice and resolution.

The Connection of Our Core Beliefs to Historical Values

- Helping Us Avoid Trouble: A very practical reason: obeying the law helps you avoid negative consequences like fines, jail time, and damage to your reputation.

When citizens stop abiding by laws, the results are serious for everyone.

- Individual Penalties: The lawbreaker faces fines, jail, and serious damage to their life and relationships.
- Societal Breakdown: If disregard for the law becomes widespread, it overwhelms law enforcement and leads to chaos, danger, and a total loss of trust between people.
- Erosion of Freedoms: As the rule of law weakens, our individual liberties are put at risk. This is how arbitrary power and oppression take hold.

Now, a quick note. Some argue that civil disobedience is sometimes necessary to challenge laws that are truly unjust and push society toward a better, more equitable place. That's a complex debate that I will save for others. The simple fact remains, if we want the benefits of a free, functional society, we must commit to respecting and abiding by its laws.

Respect the Rights, Reliefs, and Opinions of Others

There are moral, philosophical, legal, and practical reasons why citizens should respect the rights, beliefs, and opinions of others. It's important to not confuse respect with agreement. We do not have to agree with someone to acknowledge and respect their right to a differing opinion. This respect is essential for a functional, peaceful, and thriving democratic society.

This topic always reminds me of a speech from the movie *The American President*.[1]

> America isn't easy. America is advanced citizenship. You got to want it bad because it's gonna put up a fight. It's gonna say, you want free speech, let's see you acknowledge a man whose words make your blood boil, who's standing center stage and advocating at the top of his lungs that what you would spend a lifetime opposing at the top of yours. You want to claim this land is the land of the free, then the symbol of your country cannot just be a flag. The symbol also has to be one of its citizens exercising his right to burn that flag in protest. Now show me that, defend that, celebrate that in your classrooms, then you can stand up and sing about the land of the free.

The reason we consistently fail to meet this democratic challenge and a huge factor contributing to the polarization we see today is that we are absolutely convinced our views are the only correct ones. We don't acknowledge or respect that others have the right to not just hold, but actually express, their own views. Instead of just accepting that someone might have a different point of view, we feel it's our mission to convince them they're wrong. It seems that most political conversations today are about convincing, not understanding This has become such a major problem that I wanted to dedicate a lot of words just digging into this specific issue.

The reasons for respecting the rights, beliefs, and opinions of our fellow citizens fall into three categories: ethical/philosophical, legal/democratic, and societal/practical.

Ethical and Philosophical Reasons

Ethical and philosophical reasons for respecting the rights, beliefs, and opinions of others include upholding our social contract, preserving inherent human dignity, and following the golden rule.

- The Social Contract: Philosophers like Thomas Hobbes and John Locke proposed that people agree to a "social contract." We cede certain rights to a governing body in exchange for protection and social order. This implies a mutual obligation among citizens to respect each other's rights to ensure the well-being of our community.
- Inherent Human Dignity: Many ethical traditions, including the Universal Declaration of Human Rights, are based on the principle that all have inherent dignity

and are equal in rights. Respecting each other's rights and beliefs acknowledges our worth as human beings.
- The Golden Rule: Okay, we all know this one. The ethical principle of treating others as we would wish to be treated is a foundational reason for respecting fellow citizens. We cannot expect others to respect our beliefs and opinions if we do not offer the same courtesy to them.

Legal and Democratic Reasons

Legal and democratic reasons for respecting the rights, beliefs, and opinions of others include providing the cornerstone of democracy, defending freedom of speech and religion, and holding our leaders accountable.

- A Cornerstone of Democracy: Respect for individual rights is fundamental to any democracy. The US Constitution and its amendments, including the Fourteenth Amendment's guarantee of equal protection, establish the legal framework for respecting our rights as citizens.
- Freedom of Speech and Religion: The First Amendment protects freedom of expression and religion. Respecting these freedoms for others is a civic duty, even when we disagree with their views. This does not mean we must agree with every opinion, but that we must acknowledge their right to hold and express it.

- Holding Leaders Accountable: A free exchange of ideas, where those with diverse viewpoints feel respected and heard, is necessary to hold officials accountable. Disregarding the opinions of others undermines the robust public discourse that allows us to question and influence our government.

Societal and Practical Reasons

Societal and practical reasons for respecting the rights, beliefs, and opinions of others include promoting social cohesion, fostering innovation and problem-solving, enhancing personal growth, and preventing cycles of disrespect.

- Promotes Social Cohesion: Respecting differences reduces conflict and builds a more cohesive society. When we feel our rights are protected, we are more likely to participate in and contribute to our communities.
- Fosters Innovation and Problem-solving: Diversity in thought and experience leads to more creative solutions and better decision-making. When different perspectives are welcomed and respected, we can tackle complex challenges more effectively.
- Enhances Personal Growth: Engaging with different viewpoints and cultures can enhance our personal growth and empathy. Exposure to new ideas helps us to challenge our assumptions and deepen our understanding of the world.

- Prevents Cycles of Disrespect: Disregarding the rights and opinions of others can create a cycle of disrespect and conflict that negatively impacts everyone. In contrast, acting with civility can allow political and social decisions to be accepted and later challenged peacefully.

Bottom line, failure to tolerate and understand the views of others keeps citizens from participating in democracy in an effective manner. Disagree without being disagreeable and honor the otherness of others.

While the foundational pledges of this second stanza define how we interact with our fellow citizens, it only represents half of our duty. The other half we define within the third stanza which involves the relentless and active work of self-governance, which should compel us to stay informed, contribute our efforts, and participate in the civic life of our nation.

Endnotes

1. Rob Reiner, The American President, Michael Douglas, Warner Brothers, Universal Pictures, Columbia Pictures, United International Pictures, 1995 (1:42).

Protecting Our Nation and Upholding Its Ideals

I am an American citizen. I stay informed of issues affecting my community and actively contribute to its well-being. I participate in the democratic process and serve in times of need.

The third stanza highlights our role in being engaged in our communities and actively participating at both local and national levels to contribute positively to its well-being. These two sentences are all about staying informed and participating; actions which are absolutely essential for a healthy democracy, building a resilient, fair, and vibrant nation for everyone.

The Power of an Informed Citizen

The Necessity of Being Informed. Knowing the facts is the best way to hold government accountable and achieve better outcomes. This goes beyond just listening to our favorite news network and reading social media feeds. It involves taking the time to understanding both sides of issues. It supports:

- Smart Decisions: Being informed empowers us to make educated choices about everything that affects us, from voting to how tax dollars are spent.
- Accountability: An informed public is the best check on government, driving our elected leaders to be transparent and helping prevent corruption.
- Combating Misinformation: Using reliable and varying sources protects us against the misinformation that fuels social division.
- Effective Response: Accurate information is vital for coordinating actions and responding effectively during times of need.

The Impact of Active Participation. Informed citizens ensure that participation is productive, and active participation ensures that civic knowledge translates into real-world accountability. Showing up translates knowledge into influence, strengthening our community and us as individuals. It brings about:

- Influence and Better Policy: Our active involvement allows us to directly influence policies and ensures diverse voices are heard, leading to fairer, more legitimate decisions and better governance.

- Stronger Bonds: Participation—through volunteering or civic groups—builds social connections and a true sense of shared purpose, which strengthens our community's ability to solve problems.
- Personal Growth and Belonging: Contributing to our community boosts self-confidence, reduces isolation, and provides a powerful sense of pride and identity. We all could use more of that.

Contributing to the Well-Being of Others and the Community

The second idea expressed within this stanza is about contributing to the well-being of others and our communities. The power of an informed citizen is not an end in itself; it is the necessary fuel that drives us to actively contribute to the well-being of others and the community. As citizens we have a vital, dual role: ensuring a responsive government and providing support to our communities and nation in times of need. Supporting our community means supporting our fellow citizens.

I've been a big fan of actor, author, and humanitarian Gary Sinise long before I met him in February 2006 when he and his Lt Dan Band played a free concert at Luke Air Force Base in Arizona, where my family and I were stationed at the time. In his book *Grateful American: A Journey from Self to Service*,[1] Gary talks about (1) a "calling to serve" beyond himself, for the greater good of our country; (2)

the importance of community and common values; and (3) the average American's tendency to take for granted the freedom and security we enjoy.

Gary, a recipient of the Presidential Citizens Medal, has lived these ideas and is a living example of exemplary service to his fellow citizens. Service is crucial in times of need because it provides practical support to those struggling, strengthens community bonds by fostering empathy and collective purpose, and offers individuals a powerful sense of fulfillment, gratitude, and personal growth. His book is an inspiring read for any American, those who are already patriotic and grateful, as well as those who are indifferent about service to our country.

Helping others when they need it is absolutely vital. It's the engine for building strong communities, fostering empathy, and genuinely improving the well-being of both the giver and the person receiving the help. This simple cycle of support is what creates a more compassionate and resilient society. The benefits of helping others are profound, affecting individuals and the entire community. For the person receiving help, it provides:

- A Safety Net: When someone is in a crisis, facing a disaster, or dealing with a personal loss, our support ensures their basic needs are met. It literally keeps them from falling further into distress.

Protecting Our Nation and Upholding Its Ideals

- Trust and Validation: Receiving help makes a person feel seen, heard, and valued. Knowing they aren't alone builds trust and is a powerful remedy for loneliness or despair.
- Restores Hope: A kind act, no matter how small, can restore a person's faith in humanity and give them the emotional boost they need to face their challenges head-on.

Contributing to the well-being of others also benefits the giver by:

- Boosting Mental Health: Studies show that helping others can reduce stress, anxiety, and depression. Our brain releases "feel-good" neurochemicals like endorphins, leading to "helper's high."
- Creating Purpose: Helping others gives our life a greater sense of meaning and fulfillment. When we see the positive impact of our actions, it reinforces our self-worth and confidence.
- Fostering Gratitude: Being aware of our ability to help gives us perspective on our own life and naturally increases a sense of gratitude for what we have.

Providing support to others also offers great benefits for our community by:

- Strengthening Connections: Acts of kindness foster trust and cooperation, deepening bonds between us and creating a more cohesive community.

- Solving Social Problems: Organized efforts, like volunteering at a local food bank or cleaning up a park, address social issues that money alone can't fix. They build resilient communities.
- Creating a Ripple Effect: Kindness is contagious. When we witness or receive generosity, we are more likely to pass that generosity on, creating a virtuous cycle of altruism.

Ultimately, helping others is the natural extension of empathy—the ability to genuinely understand and share the feelings of others. It's the most tangible way we can act on our compassion. Empathy is the gateway to action. While empathy is the emotional understanding, compassion adds the desire to take action to alleviate the someone's suffering. It creates stronger relationships. Practicing empathy and compassion allows for deeper connections and a greater understanding of what others are experiencing, leading to more meaningful and impactful help that strengthens our communities.

Participating In Our Democracy

The third concept within this stanza is participation in our democracy. Active participation in our democracy is essential for having a government that actually works for us. It's what holds elected officials accountable. It's about so much more than just casting a vote. Civic engagement

Protecting Our Nation and Upholding Its Ideals

builds trust and legitimacy in the very institutions that govern us.

Why You Need to Get Involved. The benefits of civic participation include:

- Influencing Policy: When we participate, we can directly influence the laws and policies that affect our lives. Without public input, legislation can have long-term, negative impacts.
- Ensuring Good Governance: Government leaders make better decisions when they have complete information and diverse perspectives from their constituents. Involving the public creates better, more resilient solutions to our toughest social problems.
- Increasing Accountability: Engagement holds public servants accountable and helps prevent corruption. Our voice, especially at the local level, can make a huge difference, as a few votes can change everything.
- Fostering Community: Working toward a common cause builds relationships, strengthens networks, and brings our diverse communities together, giving individuals a real sense of purpose.
- Promoting Fairness: When certain groups don't participate, policies often ignore their needs. Higher participation rates among these groups can shift the balance of power toward more equitable outcomes.

Douglas M. Hammer

The Cost of Checking Out. To truly grasp the importance of participation, we need to confront the inevitable consequences and heavy cost of simply walking away. When we disengage from the democratic process, it leads to serious negative consequences such as:

- Skewed Policy Outcomes: Low voter turnout often means that wealthier, older populations are the ones electing our leaders. This can result in policies that ignore the wishes of large segments of the population.
- Erosion of Trust: When leaders are elected by a small percentage of voters, it undermines democracy's representativeness. We feel less connected, and trust in our system erodes.
- Vulnerability to Special Interests: Low engagement leaves our democracy open to an environment where special interests dominate the political process and block popular reforms that would benefit the public.

How to Participate Beyond Voting. The critical path to avoiding the high cost of disengagement is recognizing that true involvement means moving beyond merely casting a vote to actively participating in our democracy. Voting is fundamental, but it's just the starting line. There are many ways we can participate to make a difference.

- Advocate: Contact your elected officials by phone or email. Stay informed and voice your opinions at local council or state government meetings.

Protecting Our Nation and Upholding Its Ideals

- Volunteer: Give your time to issue-based organizations. Join community groups, volunteer for local initiatives, or start grassroots movement in your neighborhoods.
- Run for Office: Consider running for a public office.
- Serve on a Jury: Uphold a basic responsibility of citizenship, supporting our legal system.

This commitment to active participation—engaging with our communities and contributing positively at both local and national levels—is the daily expression of our citizenship. It is this profound and active role as Americans that now compels us toward a final, unified declaration of our loyalty and our enduring commitment to our country and every fellow citizen.

Endnotes

1. Grateful American: A Journey from Self to Service by Gary Sinise, with Marcus Brotherton Nashville, Tennessee: Nelson Books, 2019. pp. 280.

Declaration of Our Commitment

I am an American citizen. Proud patriot and protector of our Constitution. I practice accountability, civility, and tolerance. I reject violence as a way of settling differences. I protect and maintain my rights by exercising my responsibilities.

The final stanza reiterates our role as Americans and concludes with strong declaration of our commitment to the country and our fellow citizens.

Practicing accountability, civility, and tolerance while rejecting violence isn't just a feel-good thing; it's absolutely essential for building healthy relationships, strong communities, and a functional America. These principles give us a constructive way to solve problems, while violence only guarantees more harm and suffering.

Douglas M. Hammer

The Power of Accountability

Accountability is the simple but powerful practice of owning our role and responsibility in a situation, especially when we've caused harm. Accountability is important because it:

- Encourages Repair and Healing: Instead of focusing on blame, accountability focuses us on acknowledging harm and working to make things right. This process helps us repair trust, deepens understanding, and allows relationships and communities to heal.
- Builds Trust: When we take responsibility for our actions, we show integrity. This fosters an environment where we feel safe and reliable, which is necessary for effective conflict resolution.
- Promotes Growth: Holding ourself accountable encourages reflection and continuous improvement. It pushes us toward constructive dialogue instead of deflecting blame.

The Importance of Civility

Taking responsibility for our own behavior is the essential first step, as true civility requires us to apply that internal accountability to how we interact with others. Civility is disagreeing without disrespect and looking for common ground as a starting point. Disagreeing without being disagreeable is a key competent to good citizenship because it:

- Facilitates Productive Communication: Civility helps us de-escalate tension by encouraging respectful listening and honest expression, even on sensitive topics. It prevents arguments from turning into hostile, unproductive shouting matches.
- Builds Mutual Respect: By treating others with courtesy, we maintain mutual respect. This allows people with wildly different perspectives to engage with one another and seek actual solutions, rather than resorting to personal attacks.
- Enables Innovation: In a civil environment, we feel safe to express ideas and challenge the status quo without fear of ridicule. That openness is crucial for innovation and creative problem-solving.

The Importance of Tolerance

While civility guides the respectful manner of our interactions, it must be paired with tolerance. Tolerance involves accepting and embracing our fellow citizens in their many forms—political, cultural, religious, ethnic, and more. Embracing tolerance:

- Reduces Conflict: Tolerance prevents the disputes that often arise from misunderstandings, prejudice, and the desire for everyone to be the same. It allows for peaceful coexistence, letting us channel our energy into positive activities.

- Strengthens Society: Tolerance encourages empathy by broadening our understanding of different perspectives. This creates a more inclusive environment where we feel valued, leading to stronger social ties and a more harmonious society.
- Builds Resilience: When we're exposed to diverse viewpoints, we develop the mental strength to navigate challenges and bounce back from adversity, which contributes to overall well-being.

It's important to spend a little more time discussing civility and tolerance because of their critical impact on good citizenship. They are the key to countering the human bias that divides us as a nation.

In his book *Decent Discourse: Saving Your Country by Loving Your (Wrong?) Neighbor*,[1] Jay Jackson discusses the importance of loving and engaging with people, particularly neighbors, who hold fundamentally different views. He advocates for a shift from seeing political rivals as enemies to recognizing them as neighbors, arguing that loving those with whom we disagree is not just a moral obligation but a necessary act to restore national unity and health. I couldn't agree more.

While civility and tolerance should guide our behavior, having meaningful conversations with people we fundamentally disagree with can feel nearly impossible. But it's vital to civil discourse. According to American activist Meagan Phelps-Roper,[2] there are four simple—

Declaration of Our Commitment

yet powerful—things we can do to make meaningful conversations possible.

1. Stop Assuming the Worst. When someone has a view we disagree with or even hate, our mind instantly assumes they're malicious. That assumption immediately shuts down our empathy. We forget they're a complex human with a whole life that shaped their beliefs. Instead, we should assume they have good or at least neutral intent. This gives our brain a better framework to start a real dialogue, instead of getting stuck in that initial wave of anger.
2. Ask Real Questions. When trying to have meaningful conversations, we shouldn't just launch into our argument. Instead, we should ask genuine questions to figure out why others believe what they do. It is impossible to make a solid counterargument if we don't actually understand other's perspective. Plus, when we ask questions, it signals that we're listening, which makes the other person feel heard and much more open to engaging.
3. Stay Calm. We all know those people who think being right justifies being rude—harsh tones, snarky comments, interruptions. But that behavior just blows up the whole discussion. It's natural to want to match the energy level of the other person, but if the conversation gets heated, refuse to escalate. Remember, volume doesn't equal comprehension. Also, while

there may be disadvantages to digital communication, there is one big advantage we can leverage: the buffer of time and space between us and the people whose ideas we find so frustrating. We can use that buffer. Instead of lashing out, we can pause, breathe, change the subject, or walk away, and then come back to it when we're ready. We're not ending the discussion, just hitting pause so we can come back to it with a clearer head.

4. Make Our Case. It's tempting to think our position is so obviously right that we shouldn't have to explain or defend it. If others don't get it, it must be their problem, right? Wrong. If it were that simple, everyone would agree. We have to remember that people's beliefs are rooted in their life experiences. If we want someone to consider changing their mind, we have to actually make the case for it; we can't expect them to spontaneously come around.

When it comes to having meaningful conversations, the good news is that these steps are simple to outline. The bad news is that they are incredibly hard to do in practice. It's tough to extend empathy and compassion to people who we feel are showing us hostility. Our righteous indignation—that seductive certainty that we are right—is a powerful force to overcome. But we have to push past it because intensifying conflict and hatred is not the future we want for ourselves, our country, or the next generation. We must choose to listen and talk, even when it's uncomfortable.

Declaration of Our Commitment

Violence as a Consequences of Rejection

We have all seen the dangerous consequences of what happens when we toss out accountability, civility, and tolerance in favor of violence, the results can be severe to include:

- Cycle of Violence: Violence never truly resolves the root cause of a conflict; it only forces action. This creates a cycle of revenge and hatred that perpetuates itself, as the impacted person or group is left with an unaltered conviction and the desire for retribution.
- Erosion of Community: When conflict is settled through violence, it destroys relationships, damages trust, and polarizes communities. This toxic environment makes future collaboration and reconciliation almost impossible.

In my mind it's clear that accountability, civility, and tolerance are the only path forward to healing the polarization we see in our country today, but these steps are only possible when we first embrace the fundamental truth that the relationship between our rights and our responsibilities is the absolute foundation of a citizenship.

Rights and Responsibilities

The relationship between our rights and our responsibilities is the absolute foundation of a working society—it's totally reciprocal.

Douglas M. Hammer

Think of it this way: rights are the freedoms guaranteed to us, while responsibilities are the duties we owe to our country and others in the community. We can't truly enjoy our rights unless we fulfill our responsibilities, because that's what ensures everyone else can enjoy theirs too. Rights and responsibilities are two sides of the same coin, essential for a fair society where everyone can thrive without infringing on the liberties of our fellow citizens.

Rights and responsibilities are interconnected. For every right we have, there is a corresponding responsibility. For example, we have the right to free speech, but that comes with the responsibility not to use it to spread intentional harm or dangerous misinformation. Responsibilities act as a necessary counterbalance to rights. They keep us from using our freedoms in a way that negatively impacts the community or violates the rights of others. To be an engaged citizen, we must grasp both. We get to enjoy our rights, but we must also fulfill our duties like obeying laws and working with others to maintain a just society. This vital connection between our rights and responsibilities is precisely why the opposing force—a mindset rooted in pure entitlement—fundamentally weakens the entire foundation of citizenship

Entitlement Weakens Society

In the introduction of this book, I mentioned that those with an entitlement view of citizenship would not likely

Declaration of Our Commitment

welcome a citizen's creed. Because of the toxic affect it can have on citizenship, I feel it's worth exploring the dangers of an entitlement mindset.

The balance between rights and responsibilities is the core of a harmonious society. It allows you to pursue your interests while making sure everyone else's well-being is considered. Unfortunately, an entitlement view—where people prioritize their wants over their obligations—causes social instability and diminishes personal growth. When we divorce rights from duties, we break down social cohesion and mutual respect.

An entitlement mindset completely erodes our sense of accountability for our own actions and failures. This erosion of personal accountability leads to:

- Blame-Shifting: When we feel entitled, we often blame others for our shortcomings, which prevents us from learning and growing.
- Reduced Motivation: When we adopt the mindset that success is an inherent right rather than an earned outcome, our inherent motivation begins to decline. An entitlement mindset alters the balance between effort and reward: if the reward is guaranteed, the struggle is rendered meaningless, and we miss the opportunity to build strength and resilience through hardship.
- Stunted Resilience: Refusing to take responsibility prevents us from evolving, hampering our ability to

problem-solve and cope with setbacks because we believe we are owed a life without struggle.

On a broader societal level, an entitlement view weakens the social contract that binds a community together. This weakening of society can manifest in the form of:

- Neglect of the Common Good: An extreme focus on individual wants leads to a decreased interest in the well-being of the broader community. This makes cooperation on shared challenges much more difficult.
- Political Polarization: Overemphasizing individual rights without acknowledging social responsibilities fuels extreme political polarization. It fosters a climate where compromise is difficult and respect for differing views is low.
- Increased Conflict: The belief that you are more deserving than others is a recipe for hostility. When people aggressively assert their rights while ignoring others', community harmony is endangered.
- Individual Impacts: For the individual, the entitlement mindset is a guarantee of chronic dissatisfaction. Exaggerated feelings of deservingness lead to high expectations that are frequently unmet. The gap between expectation and reality causes constant disappointment and unhappiness. This often leads to increased anger. When a person's perceived rights are challenged, their anger and hostility intensify as they defend their inflated claims.

Declaration of Our Commitment

Practicing accountability, civility, and tolerance while rejecting violence and exercising our responsibilities isn't just a list of good behaviors —it's the bedrock of good citizenship. Why? Because these actions are what build a stable, functional, and prosperous community and country. These virtues are the foundation of a healthy democracy, allowing us to resolve conflicts peacefully, respect different viewpoints, and work together toward the common good. They are what make our system work.

Endnotes

1. Jackson, Jay. Decent Discourse: Saving Your Country by Loving Your (Wrong?) Neighbor. Decent Discourse Press, 2022

2. Phelps-Roper, M. (2017, March). I grew up in the Westboro Baptist Church. Here's why I left [Video]. TED Conferences. https://www.ted.com/talks/megan_phelps_roper_i_grew_up_in_the_westboro_baptist_church_here_s_why_i_left

Wrap-up

Freedom is a gift from our founding fathers, but they recognized maintaining it would be a struggle. On July 3, 1776, John Adams famously wrote a letter to his wife, Abigail, reflecting on the Declaration of Independence. He predicted the long struggle ahead, stating, "I am well aware of the toil and blood and treasure, that it will cost us to maintain this Declaration, and support and defend these States."

The "us" John Adams was referring to was the everyday citizen. In order to keep our freedom, we, as citizens, need to make maintenance our absolute focus. We must heed President Ronald Reagan's warning that:

> Freedom is never more than one generation away from extinction. We didn't pass it on to our children in the bloodstream. The only way they can inherit the freedom we have known is if we fight for it, protect it, defend it, and then hand it to them with the well-fought lessons of how they

> in their lifetime must do the same. And if you and
> I don't do this, then you and I may well spend our
> sunset years telling our children and our children's
> children what it once was like in America when
> men were free.

Good citizenship is the only thing that keeps a democracy working. It ensures we stay involved, make informed choices, and protect the shared values that stop our government from losing its accountability to us. A healthy democracy isn't a spectator sport; it relies on the consistent effort and civic engagement of its citizens to truly thrive. Our vast rights are a gift, and they demand something in return—a sense of responsibility, not entitlement. This urgency to define our civic duty stems from a deep love of freedom and the clear, current warning that liberty is fragile.

Just look at America today. We are deeply polarized—divided by where we live, what we believe, and who we vote for—and this division has shattered social trust. The terrifying consequence of this division is the surge in violence. To address this crisis, we must have a firm anchor against hateful and divisive acts. While political leaders often make this divide worse, we, as citizens, must take responsibility for bridging the gap by focusing on those qualities and beliefs that we share.

Wrap-up

We need a unifying statement to support our increased civic engagement. That's where a creed comes in. *The American Citizen's Creed* attempts to define the shared traits every US citizen should aspire to embody in those 110 words. Ultimately, the entire creed hinges on the reciprocal relationship between rights and responsibilities. Our rights can only be protected if we fulfill our duties to the community, making the active exercise of responsibility the non-negotiable final declaration of citizenship through our creed.

Our pride in being an American citizen should not be rooted in a mere birthright or a completed naturalization process, but rather in knowing we are actively living by the enduring tenets of *The American Citizen's Creed*. Being a citizen is not a passive title; it is an ongoing commitment.

I'm unapologetically proud to be a citizen of our great country and hope you will join me in demonstrating that pride through our actions every single day.

Quotes on Citizenship

I love a good quote. Here are some of my favorites from our presidents around the concept of citizenship.

Born in other countries, yet believing you could be happy in this, our laws acknowledge, as they should do, your right to join us in society, conforming, as I doubt not you will do, to our established rules. That these rules shall be as equal as prudential considerations will admit, will certainly be the aim of our legislatures, general and particular.

- President Thomas Jefferson, 1801

We must support our rights or lose our character, and with it, perhaps, our liberties. A people who fail to do it can scarcely be said to hold a place among independent nations. National honor is national property of the highest value. The sentiment in the mind of every citizen is national strength. It ought therefore to be cherished.

- President James Monroe, 1817

Douglas M. Hammer

Connected, as the Union is, with the remembrance of past happiness, the sense of present blessings, and the hope of future peace and prosperity, every dictate of wisdom, every feeling of duty, and every emotion of patriotism tend to inspire fidelity and devotion to it and admonish us cautiously to avoid any unnecessary controversy which can either endanger it or impair its strength, the chief element of which is to be found in the regard and affection of the people for each other.

- President Zachary Taylor, 1850

No citizen of our country should permit himself to forget that he is a part of its Government and entitled to be heard in the determination of its policy and its measures, and that therefore the highest considerations of personal honor and patriotism require him to maintain by whatever of power or influence he may possess the integrity of the laws of the Republic.

- President Franklin Pierce, 1856

Heretofore we have welcomed all who came to us from other lands except those whose moral or physical condition or history threatened danger to our national welfare and safety. Relying upon the zealous watchfulness of our people to prevent injury to our political and social fabric, we have encouraged those coming from foreign countries to cast their lot with us and join in the development of our vast domain, securing in return a share in the blessings of American citizenship.

- President Grover Cleveland, 1897

We accept the man as a citizen without any knowledge of his fitness, and he assumes the duties of citizenship without any knowledge as to what they are. The privileges of American citizenship are so great and its duties so grave that we may well insist upon a good knowledge of every person applying for citizenship and a good knowledge by him of our institutions. We should not cease to be hospitable to immigration, but we should cease to be careless as to the character of it. There are men of all races, even the best, whose coming is necessarily a burden upon our public revenues or a threat to social order. These should be identified and excluded.

- President Benjamin Harrison, 1899

There are some national questions in the solution of which patriotism should exclude partisanship. Magnifying their difficulties will not take them off our hands nor facilitate their adjustment. Distrust of the capacity, integrity, and high purposes of the American people will not be an inspiring theme for future political contests. Dark pictures and gloomy forebodings are worse than useless. These only becloud, they do not help to point the way of safety and honor.

> - President William McKinley, 1901

We are all of us Americans, and nothing else; we all have equal rights and equal obligations; we form part of one people, in the face of all other nations, paying allegiance only to one flag; and a wrong to any one of us is a wrong to all the rest of us.

> - President Theodore Roosevelt, 1917

This is the only country in the world which experiences this constant and repeated rebirth. Other countries depend upon the multiplication of their own native people. This country is constantly drinking strength out of new sources by the voluntary association with it of great bodies of strong men and forward-looking women out of other lands. And so by the gift of the free will of independent people it is being constantly renewed from generation to generation by the same process by which it was originally created....You have just taken an oath of allegiance to the United States. Of allegiance to whom? Of allegiance to no one, unless it is God—certainly not of allegiance to those who temporarily represent this great Government. You have taken an oath of allegiance to a great ideal, to a great body of principles, to a great hope of the human race."

Quotes on Citizenship

"We came to America, either ourselves or in the persons of our ancestors, to better the ideals of men, to make them see finer things than they had seen before, to get rid of the things that divide and to make sure of the things that unite.

- President Woodrow Wilson, 1915

American citizenship is a high estate. He who holds it is the peer of kings. It has been secured only by untold toil and effort. It will be maintained by no other method. It demands the best that men and women have to give. But it likewise awards its partakers the best that there is on earth.

- President Calvin Coolidge, 1924

Whether one traces his Americanism back three centuries to the Mayflower, or three years to the steerage, is not half so important as whether his Americanism of today is real and genuine. No matter by what various crafts we came here, we are all now in the same boat.

- President Calvin Coolidge, 1924

The principle on which this country was founded and by which it has always been governed is that Americanism is a matter of the mind and heart; Americanism is not, and never was, a matter of race and ancestry. A good American is one who is loyal to this country and to our creed of liberty and democracy.

> - President Franklin D. Roosevelt, 1943

A people that values its privileges above its principles soon loses both.

> - President Dwight D. Eisenhower, 1953

Our citizens—naturalized or native-born—must also seek to refresh and improve their knowledge of how our government operates under the Constitution and how they can participate in it. Only in this way can they assume the full responsibilities of citizenship and make our government more truly of, by, and for the people.

> - President Lyndon B. Johnson, 1967

United States citizenship, then, is also demanding. But the demands are more than matched by the benefits. Each citizen can help himself, his fellow citizens, and his nation if he takes some time out of his life to read and talk and think about the Constitution.

> - President Richard Nixon, 1969

In a few days I will lay down my official responsibilities in this office, to take up once more the only title in our democracy superior to that of President, the title of citizen.

- President Jimmy Carter, 1981

It's long been my belief that America is a chosen place, a rich and fertile continent placed by some Divine Providence here between the two great oceans, and only those who really wanted to get here would get here. Only those who most yearned for freedom would make the terrible trek that it took to get here. America has drawn the stoutest hearts from every corner of the world, from every nation of the world. And that was lucky for America, because if it was going to endure and grow and protect its freedoms for 200 years, it was going to need stout hearts.

- President Ronald Reagan, 1990

Together as citizens we must recommit ourselves to the general duties of citizenship. Not just immigrants, but every American should know what's in our Constitution and understand our shared history. Not just immigrants, but every American should participate in our democracy by voting, by volunteering and by running for office. Not just immigrants, but every American, on our campuses and in our communities, should serve—community service breeds good citizenship. And not just immigrants, but every American should reject identity politics that seeks to separate us, not bring us together.

> - President William J. Clinton, 1998

America has never been united by blood or birth or soil. We are bound by ideals that move us beyond our backgrounds, lift us above our interests and teach us what it means to be citizens. Every child must be taught these principles. Every citizen must uphold them. And every immigrant, by embracing these ideals, makes our country more, not less, American.

> - President George W. Bush, 2001

America's welcoming society is more than a cultural tradition; it is a fundamental promise of our democracy. Our Constitution does not limit citizenship by background or birth. Instead, our nation is bound together by a shared love of liberty and a conviction that all people are created with dignity and value. Through the generations, Americans have upheld that vision by welcoming new citizens from across the globe—and that has made us stand apart.

> - President George W. Bush, 2006

As Americans, and American citizens, we are bound together in love, and loyalty, and friendship, and affection.

We must look out for each other, care for each other, and always act in the best interests of our nation and all citizens living here today. We love each other. We're proud of each other.

- President Donald J Trump, 2019

There is one thing that does define us a country: We were founded on an idea that, We hold these truths to be self-evident, that all men and women are created equal… endowed by their Creator with certain unalienable Rights… Life, Liberty, and the pursuit of Happiness. It sounds corny to Americans, as we learn this in grade school and high school. We've never fully lived up to it, but we've never, ever, ever walked away from it. Every generation opens that aperture a little bit wider.

- President Joseph Biden, 2021

As long as the American people hold in their hearts deep and devoted love of country, then there is nothing that this nation cannot achieve. Our communities will flourish. Our people will be prosperous. Our traditions will be cherished. Our faith will be strong. And our future will be brighter than ever before.

- President Donald J Trump, 2021

About the Author

Douglas Hammer is a retired US Air Force colonel with over 26 years of decorated service. Having led airmen on the front lines in Operations DESERT SHIELD/STORM and IRAQI/ENDURING FREEDOM, he witnessed firsthand the unifying power of a common code, such as the US Air Force *Airman's Creed*, during the most difficult times.

After retiring in 2014, his career of leadership and vision continued in the private sector, focusing on building high-performance cultures. *The American Citizen's Creed* is the culmination of his life's work: a powerful and necessary text born of a veteran's lifelong passion offering a concise, nonpartisan standard to help America become the best version of itself.

www.ingramcontent.com/pod-product-compliance
Lightning Source LLC
Chambersburg PA
CBHW052033030426
42337CB00027B/4982